THIS BOOK BELONGS TO:

HALLOWEEN
COLORING BOOK FOR KIDS

Copyright@2020

All Rights Reserved.

You're Magical

You're Magical

You're Magical

You're Magical

You're Magical

You're Magical

You're Magical

You're Magical

You're Magical

You're Magical

You're Magical

You're Magical

You're Magical

You're Magical

You're Magical

You're Magical

You're Magical

You're Magical

You're Magical

You're Magical

You're Magical

You're Magical

You're Magical

You're Magical

You're Magical

You're Magical

You're Magical

You're Magical

You're Magical

You're Magical

You're Magical

You're Magical

You're Magical

You're Magical

You're Magical

You're Magical

You're Magical

You're Magical

You're Magical

You're Magical

You're Magical

You're Magical

You're Magical

You're Magical

You're Magical

You're Magical

You're Magical

You're Magical

Made in the USA
Las Vegas, NV
05 October 2021